CU00403540

The Best Things in Life Are Free

Published by Green Dragon Publishing
PO Box 375, Lymington SO41 1AQ

Text copyright © Ian Corrie Hill 2002, 2011
Illustrations by Rosemary Taylor

The rights of Ian Corrie Hill to be identified as the author of
this work has been asserted.

Green Dragon Publishing is a small business specialising in
the publication of fiction linked to ecology, the natural world
and our relationship with the creatures who share it.

Printed in Totton, Hampshire by Hobbs the Printers Limited

MIX
Paper from
responsible sources
FSC® C020438
FSC
www.fsc.org

1 3 5 7 9 10 8 6 4 2

A catalogue record for this book is available from the British
Library
ISBN: 978-0-9563945-2-1

The Best Things in Life are Free

By Ian Corrie Hill

Sketches by Rosemary Taylor

Green Dragon Publishing

www.greendragonpublishing.co.uk

This little book would never have been published without the help of Melanie Newman, who is also a good neighbour.

Part One: If Dreams Come True

Part Two: Country Love

To my youngest daughter
Nicola

Cancer so often strikes a seemingly healthy person and the trauma also affects the whole family.

Various charities and hospices are doing wonderful work but much more research is needed to prevent the disease. By giving the proceeds to Cancer Research UK, I hope that in a tiny way this little book may help.

Ian

Part Three: Striving to Some Purpose

When the Light Fails
The Long Night Ahead
The Army
One Word – One God
The Best Seller
Graduation Day
Hindsight

Part Four: Sentimental Journey

Who Would Be So Lucky?
The Pinnacles of Life
A Friend for Life
Reverie
A Heady Wine
Songs in One's Time
Whisper on the Village Green
Fate

Part One

If Dreams Come True

For One Moment

Remember a full moon one July?
High on a hillside, just you and me
Scattered harbour lights far below
On a velvet bed of Eastern sea

There was a question, crucial to your life
Out of the blue; could I really be his wife?
For a minute your head said, wait and think
Though your heart knew the answer in an eyelid's blink

The scene was set, the players on stage
A romance from the opening page
We kissed underneath a roof of stars
For that moment the world was ours.

Hong Kong 15-7-1954

Skye Dreams

First light steals over Isle Ornsay,
Silver moon mirrored in a placid sea,
Crimson sky blushes through clouds of grey,
Highland hills far as an eye can see.

Cottages washed white amid the bracken,
Purple heather and granite on the hill,
Trickling burns that never slacken,
In a hundred years they'll be there still.

There's a pin drop stillness but for the sheep,
Calling from the hill while the village sleeps,
Lord cast a spell on this idyllic scene,
While I may fantasise the life I dream.

It's time I lit the peat fire in the grate,
Pull on my boots and stroll round the estate,
Take the dogs; find something for the pot,
Brace of grouse or brown trout from the loch.

Maybe I'll take the horse across the moor,
Canter down the track to the shore,
Then I'll board the yacht anchored in the bay,
Raise the jib, slip the moorings, and steal away.

Sea View

Dawn, sea and sand, far out on the seaweed rocks,
Eastern sky shimmers a golden path,
Through the anchored yachts,
Quiet but for a gull's searching cry
And ripples of the turning tide.

By stealth some unseen hand has drowned the rocks,
Changing the view, but darling where are you?

Dozing still, in a rumpled heap,
Of hair, sheet, a pair of feet,
"Nice cup of tea – lovely day."
Moan, roll over: "Go away!"

Time was she'd go, hand in mine,
To watch the dawn sun rise,
Kiss the dew from my lips
And gaze into my eyes.

The view was even better then,
Not long had we been wed,
As the tide flooded in again,
She'd take me back to bed.

Seaview, Isle of Wight

Night Travel

Nightfall when the world's asleep,
I may take one gigantic leap,
To reach the stars that prick the night,
Sprinkled tiny diamond lights, on a jeweller's velvet cloth,
Waiting some slender finger's choice,
To sparkle in a pretty ear, like yours my dear.

I may fly across the firmament,
Through a wilderness of honeyed dreams,
And laze in those Elysian Fields,
Where angels bathe in crystal streams
Past Venus and the Milky Way,
To find the star that's guided me,
Who knew my birth, now knows my fate,
Tell me now – or am I too late?

Will my starry host invite me to the moon?
To bask within its silver stare,
Eat a slice of honey melon dew,
Turn my money over when it's new,
Or find it's only made of cheese,
And cows are jumping over
Fields of buttercups and clover.

Ski down the airways of the night,
Pursued by thundering nimbus hordes,
Where piles of white wool cumulus,
Build castles for Utopian lords,
Spin round the dark side of the sun,
Hurry through stratospheric rings,
Before the dawn breaks
And sunrise scorches my wings.

Continents and seas rush up to meet me,
City streets sparkle below,
I'm tired of travelling on my own.
Will your blue eyes be there to greet me?
I love you darling, I'm coming home.

(Sketch by Anne Moxom)

The Lakes

Green upon green upon green,
Is this paradise I've seen?
Where from some dusty foreign parts you dream,
Of England's flowered grass and watered scene?

Lakeland fells sweep down to rest,
Reflections shine in waters still,
Or ruffled grey and empty left,
When the wind blows ill.

Cattle grazing in the dales,
By dry stone walls and nestled farm,
Remembered toys of childhood,
Green pastures of a quiet psalm,
There's bluebells in the wild wood.

Nab scar hangs over Rydal water,
Go in Spring to Dora's field,
Daffodils for a poet's daughter,
Pray in church where Wordsworth kneeled.

Sourmilk Gill by Bleaberry Tarn,
Names to conjure, views to thrill,
Wrynose Bottom to Hardknot Pass,
Langdale Pykes over Dungeon Gill.

Tranquil tarns in their glassy sleep,
Crag, scar, pike, mirrored in the deep,
Iris, yellow flag and bog bean
Thrive in the shallows of the stream.

When the mist drifts down, silence dwells,
Just plaintive cries of sheep on the fells,
Moorhens dabble, herons are fishing,
Here you find your dreams for wishing.

The Enigma

Enigmatic cat,
Sitting on my lap,
What are you thinking?
Green eyes unblinking,
Staring straight through me,
Is she fond of me?
Not that I can see,
So inscrutable,
Indisputable,
That I'm a flattered fool,
Made use of, as a rule,
While I stroke, she will purr,
That is all I get from her.

She takes advantage of me,
Because she knows I'm weak.
I'll never know she loves me;
If only she could speak.

One day she'll fail to wake,
And I will shed a tear.
Did she have a heart to break?
Or anything to fear?
But should I go before her,
Will she climb up on my chair,
Sad that I'm no longer there?

There's another kingdom in the sky,
Where we will meet again some day,
Perhaps then she'll have a tongue to speak,
And give the answers that I seek,
"Of course I always loved you",
"It's only you that I adore."
While I lie mute and glowing,
Doing nothing anymore,
Except those things that suit me,
While she strokes me with her paw.

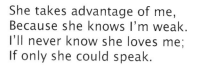

The Stranger

They found the body in the heather,
By the old drovers' road to the Isles,
He lay in soft shoes and city clothes,
No rucksack betrayed his purpose,
So incongruous it seemed in the sunlight,
Cotton-grass stirring in a gentle breeze,
But the nights are cold on the hills,
When the temperature drops to a freeze.

Was he alone in the fading moments?
While a chill mist crept off the moor,
Wrapped in his arms, knees to chin,
As once in the warmth of the womb,
His life slipping away in the dark,
In the glint of the watching moon.

They fetched him down on a highland garron;
To the kirk in the valley below,
No labels were found on his clothes,
They emptied his pockets, nothing was there,
But sewn into the breast of his nondescript shirt,
They found some pieces of auburn hair.

"Hypothermia" they said at the mortuary,
Of his origins there was no clue,
But by chance they found a small key,
In a hollow in the heel of his shoe.

Much was written in the local press,
Police notified Interpol,
But he'd covered his tracks well,
His mission aborted, no one reported
And still there's a story to tell.

One year to the day, a cairn appeared
On the lonely spot where he died.
No one's come forward to honour his name,
But some day she'll come to claim the key,
I write from the grave – the stranger was me.

The Highland Burn

In the heather by a highland burn,
Breathing the peace we strive to earn,
Water trickles in the quietude,
Lonely wind stirs the solitude.

Time stands still, for this sensation,
Murmuring voices haunt the moor,
Water's whispered conversation,
Spirits howl when the wind is raw.

Ice blue loch stares vacant at the skies,
Only a ripple as brown trout rise,
Black corries that never see the sun,
Crevice, granite rocks, white waters run.

Purple hills reach to a cloudy sky,
Lay me to my rest here, when I die,
When the light has failed for all of us,
These hills still stand when our bones are dust,
The same sweet music of the falling burn,
Calls our care free spirits to return.

Corrour
August 1990

Part Two

Country Love

Forest Stream

Life of a forest stream is fickle,
Down to a trickle in a long hot summer,
Drowned in bed when the rains outnumber,
Willow saplings careless grow, choking the flow,
Birch, hazel, alder, lean and overgrow.

Random along the water's edge;
Marestail with water parsnip creep,
Marsh marigold and bottle sedge,
Fools watercress mix meadowsweet.

Sedge warblers, buntings in the rushes,
Rare brilliance of the fisher kings,
In spring a pair of mallard flushes,
Shy heron's slow retreating wings.

Skittering sedgeflies, water boatmen,
Beetles, newts, frogs and spiders,
Wriggling, hopping, swimming creatures,
Beloved of natural history teachers.

While the watchers watch with fond emotion,
Our children's children will still build dams,
To try to halt perpetual motion,
Float sticks beneath the old footbridge,
Downstream emerge the other side,
To shrill with little infant's pride,
And where the meander water's slack,
Small boys still net the stickleback.

(North Weirs, New Forest)

Old Farm Days

In days gone by, the countryside,
Ploughed brown, sown green or yellow corn,
Good land was never 'set aside',
Before the motorway was born.
Farms were farms, not camping sites,
Butter was good for appetites,
No one asked for subsidy,
Cows milked by hand, hens ranged free.

Hawthorn, Blackthorn, cut and laid,
Hedgerows for wildlife made,
Haystacks to find needles in,
Leather harness, brass and tin,
Milk churns waiting silver clean,
Farmer's wife has skimmed the cream.

Cottage cob with moss grown thatch,
Sweet peas, beans and cabbage patch,
Lean-to sheds down rutty tracks,
Binder twine, old gunny sacks,
Rusty plough in nettle bed,
No one mourns the life it led.

Summer harvest, up since dawn,
Weary arms from scything corn,
Aching backs from tossing hay,
Praying that the sun will stay,
Bread and cheese with cider lunch,
Hear the horse's nosebag munch.

Heavy horse clink, clip and clop,
Straw in mouth, farm boy on top,
Dobbin, docile, patient, strong,
"Git up!", "Whoa boy!" all day long.

Cut and turn, bind, stook and stack,
Ferrets wriggling in the sack,
Rabbits bolting through the stubble,
Busy terriers, seeking trouble.

Pitch the sheaves up on the cart,
Horse drawn, never fails to start,
Last gathered in the setting sun,
A jug of ale, the day's work done.

Harvest Sunday, church adorn,
Fruit and veg with sheaves of corn,
Singing how we ploughed and scattered,
Things in life that really mattered.

Barns empty now and stubble burns,
For old farm days there's no return,
But sweet dry scent of fresh cut hay,
Make memories seem like yesterday,
Our daily bread was truly earned,
When wheels and life more slowly turned.

(Worcestershire boyhood memories)

Hedgerows

Hedgerows, ribs of the ancient countryside,
Wreathed in sweet briar, dogwood, traveller's joy,
Sheltered havens where small mammals hide,
Blackberry picking when I was a boy.

Songbirds born to this spiky, tangled world,
Before dogrose, and elderflower unfold,
Come autumn, hips and haws, old man's beard,
Leave empty nurseries where young birds reared.

Hawthorn, blackthorn keep the cattle in,
Red berries for the birds, sloes for gin,
Home for wood beetles, hedgehogs, shy voles,
Miniature jungle our cat patrols.

The hidden world of the hedgerow bottom,
Moss covered debris, brambles and thorn,
If we don't preserve will be forgotten,
And wildlife there will never be born.

Wild Flower Meadow

Hay meadow in an English summer,
Quaking grass heads quiver at their ease,
Grown slender after winter's slumber,
Nodding to a scented summer breeze.

Winter's scene was brown and fallow,
Now wild with cowslips, feverfew,
Purple loosestrife, pink musk mallow,
White campion, larkspur, cornflower blue.

Knapweed, leaf green purple crown,
Why cruelly named so sour?
Rich hue of a bishop's gown,
Beautiful as any flower.

Cornfield strips untouched by the farmer's spray,
Reminders of fields in a bygone day,
Scattered poppies, blood spots among the grain,
For those that never saw wild flowers again.

Self-seeded fox-named, bell-shaped glove,
Epitome of wild things I love,
Yellow rattle, scented chamomile,
Dressed so pretty does the country smile.

Whose green fingers designed each petal?
Jewelled highlights among the grasses,
Where butterflies and bees will settle,
No cultivated scene surpasses.

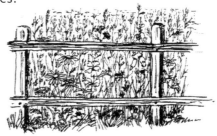

Summer

Curtain rises red, a summer dawn.
Early sun-thrown shadows on the lawn,
Dew glistening damp on the grass,
Young birds attending singing class.

Cows ambling by to milk,
Sun on cobwebs spun like silk,
Over rooftops, across the fields,
First light of morning gently steals.

Swallows nesting beneath our eaves,
Their flying lessons passed with ease,
Aerobatics around the house,
Before they take the long flight South.

Flowered perfumes, born on the breeze,
Honeysuckle, rose, bonny sweet peas,
Lavender, lilac, fresh cut grass,
Brushing the senses as you pass.

Far distant, faint, a cuckoo calls,
Oh how that wistful sound recalls,
Those balmy summers, sunshine haze,
Petals on the lawn, deckchair days,
Pink blossom falling from the trees,
Contented humming of the bees.

Winter Dawn

Winter morning's grip at dawn,
Faint light East, frost nips the air,
Crisp white carpet on the lawn,
Listen for the quietness there.

Oak tree branches, witches fingers,
Claw the sky while dusk still lingers,
Last of the stars blinks out of sight,
Black shapes are turning grey,
Crawking crows are taking flight,
How I love this time of day.

Wood pigeon woos the morning air,
Like comfort known within the womb,
Before the day's begun to care,
From sorrow, stress of life immune.

Breathe deep this peace no money can buy,
Kiss fresh thy cheek the untainted air,
Darling, would that you were here to share,
My winter morning love affair.

Song of the Fishing Reel

Fishing for dreams, highland lochs and streams
Where stone dykes climb heather bracken hills
Trout rings rise under grey cloud skies
While salmon lie low at the river bends
Or tantalise, jumping before your eyes.

Will a 'Peter Ross' make the salmon cross?
'Grouse and Claret' suit the brown trout pallet?
'Greenwell', 'Butcher', 'Olive Dun'.
What will tempt in the waters run?

Change your fly, steady nimble fingers
Cast out and draw, time has no mean
Hope still springs while daylight lingers
Here in your heart contentment feel
To the easy song of the fishing reel.

(Scotland August 2001)

No Going Back (Dalnessie, Sutherland)

I know a track that skirts the fields
Where seed plough tills and barley yields
Across the burn onto the moor
Where blackface run and buzzards soar.

To distant Corrie, green graze square
Deserted house, hollow eyes stare
Stone dyke circle once gathered sheep
None there to count, now bracken deep
Thistle grown bothy where shepherd dogs lay
Whistle in the wind, they're up and away
Gone to their rest, deep in the peat
Tired old collies, their last long sleep.

Long gone past down that moorland track
When all you had was the pack on your back,
Your dogs and ewes grazing the moor
Sunrise to sundown, life was raw
Hard days, foul nights, all shepherds know
Lambs lost to fox and corbie crow.

The moor its silent counsel keeps
Unfazed by those who come and go
Long after all the joys we seek
Same earth, same sky, same winds will blow.

No one now travels the moorland track
Silhouette by the moon, on frost chill nights
There's peat fire smoke from the chimney stack
And a lantern light to call you back
Where once was a life; but there's no going back.

A Man with No Face

By a path through the woods on the edge of the moor,
Where once was a scene to die for,
There's an overgrown bench, a forgotten view
With only ghosts from the past to sigh for.

Made of oak inscribed 'Jim loved this view 1887-1962'
Now brambles, bracken invade this place,
Hazel and hawthorn have stolen the view,
He'd weep in heaven if ever he knew.

At twilight, when birds fly home to roost,
When the fox stirs his bushy tail
And rabbits run to their burrows,
You may hear whispers on the wind,
Thin whistle through the trees,
A bustle in the thicket,
But there's no one there who sees.

When spirits return they see only the past,
So the beauty they left behind will last,
They'll never know the changes that grow,
As the years pass by, there's no one to cry,
For this tangledown, lonely, forgotten place,
That once knew the soul of the man with no face.

Part Three

Striving to Some Purpose

When the Light Fails

Turn out the light, stand in the dark,
Try to go round the room,
You'll bump into things, crack your shins,
Furniture gets in the way,
That's how it feels when the devil deals
And your sight is ebbing away.

When you can't see the sun for the mist
And the colours in flowers turn grey,
You long for the beautiful things that you miss
And you can't tell the time of the day.

What in the world would I give to see,
Snowflakes fall, a Christmas tree,
But I've no more to give, and money can't buy,
A sunrise in spring or stars in the sky.

Now I see through my memories, they don't fade,
Places and people, the tunes they played,
These twilight years dependent on others,
A child once again, my hand in my mother's.

(Sketch by Anne Moxom)

The Long Night Ahead

There would be a long night ahead,
But I did not know it when I got out of bed,

I looked through the window,
Grey mist obscured the morning,
Red showing in the East,
But I did not heed the warning.

Junk mail thudded to the floor,
One letter, the writing unclear,
I held it up to the light,
Felt a moment's pang of fear.

Down to the surgery,
"Doc, my eyes are rather blurred."
"You must see a specialist,"
I'll phone him up at once,
Don't drive your car or go too far,
Take these drops – see you in a month."

Cross over to the chemist,
Uneasy in my mind,
Children cycle by to school,
"Look out there! Are you blind?"

Safely home; greeting dogs,
Where is our morning walk?
They have seen the rising sun,
If only they could talk,
First must find that magnifier,
Lying dusty in some drawer,
How could I know I'd need it?
As Grandpa did before.

Telephone's been ringing,
Word has got around,
Would I need a white stick?
A talking book's been found.

Longest day in a lifetime,
When I climbed into bed,
Lord, give me courage,
For the long night ahead.

"Goodnight. Leave the light on in the hall."
As I remember when we were young,
Yesterday was a world away, I didn't have a care,
Now, suddenly, it is the dark again I have to fear.

The Army

In a world of prejudice and strife,
Some Christian soldiers march, but not to war,
They fight for the losers in this life
As Jesus went among the weak and poor

In dark corners and back streets of the world
Where blind eyes turn and pass the other side
They judge not why, compassion their only guide
Wherever their joyful bands are heard
Their humble mission proved by deed not word

So fall in step and march, banners flying proud
Their trumpet calls for good we should all espouse
Join them in their mercy if only just one day
Comfort for a moment someone along your way.

One Word – One God

So many faiths round the world to choose,
So many wars to see whose is best,
One word, the answer above the rest,
GOOD is one God all can believe.
Every religion can perceive,
Whenever there's truth God is there,
If there is hope God will be near,
God is love, for all to share,
And be within us when we choose,
By thoughts and deeds for others' needs.

If GOOD is God, all Gods are good,
Does it matter which we choose?
Hold your belief but don't impose,
Each man will gather what he sows.

"I valued the belief I was taught but never found the answers I sought."

The Best Seller

I have a soul too,
May not breathe the air as you do,
But I too set out with aspirations,
Conceived by love and inspiration,
Clothed with hope, hard back, letters gold,
Seeking fame, Hatchard's window,
Critics' acclaim, coffee tables grace
But I've dwelt only in the shadows
Never see the sun upon my face.

Worse than hate, indifference to your soul,
Cast out with common paperbacks
Village fetes or jumble sales,
Money for the church or saving whales.

But wait! Ten pence to catch the eye,
A gentleman; a gap to fill
On splendid shelves where I belong
With others of my background, it can't be wrong.

This story ending, bitter sweet,
Longing to be opened and enthral,
But only dusted, once a year, that's all,
My gold title, my epitaph,
Don't you laugh! I have my pride,
I rest in style and comfort now
With Shakespeare, Dickens either side.

Graduation Day

Graduation day. Proud parents attend,
Plaudits from the crowd,
Congratulations from every friend,
Further honours beckon,
Basking in the sunlight of success.

Watching in the shadows
Unnoticed, quietly satisfied,
Where no limelight shines,
They taught; not just the lines
But engaged the minds,
Encouraged, praised, inspired,
Even the most modest talent
To find the pleasures of achievement.

What a gift, what a legacy to leave,
Unsung, mostly forgotten now
But now and then fondly remembered
Long after the inspiration served its time.

(A little tribute to Rosemary and Richard Taylor)

Hindsight

"I'd do it all again,
I wouldn't change a thing",
The famous man would say,
Talking to reporters of the day.

How grand to stroll through life,
Confident that all you say and do,
Is good and true,
No second thoughts or lingering doubts,
Nothing you are not proud about,
Do these paragons in private moments,
Ever doubt themselves and make atonement,
Or do they leave it much too late,
And answer at St Peter's Gate.

For us ordinary folk,
Regrets there surely are a few,
Unkind, ill-natured things,
That is was wrong to do,
Trivial then it may have seemed,
But at the time had no appeal,
To those that suffered needlessly,
For pardon now you'd gladly kneel.

Old memories are sometimes fudged,
By seeds of doubt the devil sows,
Unlike the great by history judged,
There's no one but your conscience knows.

When the credits exceed the debits,
And you've helped someone along the way,
Contented is the man who finds his earthly dream,
Who at the end owes nothing to no one,
And the balance sheet is clean.

Play the hand you're dealt, the rest is fate,
We strive, we dream, we love, we hate,
With hindsight, we'd be kinder, wiser,
This life is but an appetiser.

Part Four

Sentimental Journey

Who would be so lucky?

Who would be so lucky coming home,
Every day rain or shine,
To a smiley face
When her eyes meet mine,
Love unspoken shines through her eyes
Unwavering, true and wise
Always there to reassure and oddly to adore
This very ordinary soul
Who needs her light and sunny touch
Which from the first I loved so much.

So many milestones passed
Long may our journey last
Darling we have come so far
Time so precious now
Each day, every hour
We found life's most precious prize
To have loved and been loved
Each day I see it in your eyes.

The Pinnacles of Life

The pinnacles of life are rare
Sweet moments when the spirits soar
Feeling that you walk on air
And the crowd's on its feet to roar.

Courting days never leave my mind
Meeting at our secret rendezvous
Precious memories still recall
The heartbeat thrill of seeing you.

Honeymooners of shy desire
Still strangers to explore
Our tenderness and passions fire
That strengthened love the more.

First born, our love conceived
Pacing the corridors and stairs
Anxious waiting for news relieved
Repeating all my silent prayers.
Your shining face, love's labour won
Your blues eyes held a mother's pride
The bundle in your arms – my son
Relief shed tears I could not hide.

Against the odds racing to win
Every nerve and sinew tried
Veins coursing with adrenaline
To get up in the final stride
Even after all these years
Still I hear the crowded cheers.

Ecstasy, life's rare sensation
We seldom reach the dizzy heights
Of starry-eyed exhilaration
Bow to applause or win the fights
Just a handful in a lifetime
Thrills that brought your heart's desire
Love or courage at the right time
Sparks that lit a roaring fire.

A Friend for Life

I have a friend who's always there
In time of trouble and despair
He listens to my every word
Even when I am absurd
Never cross should I be late
Doesn't know what it is to hate.

I've never known him let me down
Like me can't stand to shop in town
Whenever we can be together
Out upon the moors and heather.

Whenever I have been away
For a week or just one day
He'll jump and shout "At last you're here!"
As if I'd been away a year.

In my polished shoes, suit and tie
He'll barely even lift his head
Just settle deeper in his bed
But pull on boots, an old brown coat
He'll rise and stretch out to the door
"This is what I'm waiting for!"

If only their lifespan equalled ours
We'd grow old together, fading flowers
Wilting in the sun, dozing by the fire
Hunting dreams to the end of the trail
Flick of the eye, last thump of the tail.

We'll meet again in heavenly hills
Lakeland scenes, purple moors, brook trout streams
Far away from our earthly ills,
Where hedgerows square the emerald fields
And bluebells catch the sunlight through the woods
Perhaps then we'll know the reasons
For all those things we never understood.

Reverie

Early morning before the dawning,
Light the fire,
Cup of tea,
Comfy in my chair,
No one else is here.

Just the dogs, noses in the grate,
They'll soon be hot dogs on a plate!
You know who, on my lap,
She loves me madly
Digs her claws, covers me in hair,
But I love to have her there.

My purring friend, the ticking clock,
My quiet home,
Where I can find the time my own,
To sit and stare, the mind to wander,
Inconsequential things to ponder,
Until through door and window sounds,
Milkman rattles on his rounds,
Songbirds swell into a chorus
Cock crows break the dawn for us.

The day's begun, birds have flown
I'm wanted on the telephone,
I'll fetch and carry, give and borrow,
Leave my reverie 'til tomorrow.

A Heady Wine

Half close your eyes
Easy in your favourite chair
Wrap you mind around in sounds
Of harmony and flair.
Woodwind, strings, brass, timpani
Flights of jazz, a symphony
Scintillating flats and sharps
Dance the acres of your heart.

Autumn's blaze, love in spring, summer sun,
Write the lyrics of the tunes we hum
Nostalgia, romance, passion sings
To paradise on swallow's wings
Or falls in tears of dew on virgin grass
Where footprints fade, as memories pass.

So, let the music play; no one can deride
This simple balm that sense decides
That we may wallow, rhapsodise
Concertos thundering oceans wide
Ballads, love songs misty-eyed
Another world out of this time
To laze and sip this heady wine.

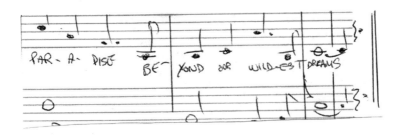

Songs in One's Time

Sung to sleep, to a mother's lullaby,
Nursery rhymes that made no sense,
Then chapel every day at school,
Tedious Te Deum as a rule.

Love songs sung in a nubile dawn,
Life was care free, come what may,
Til one day, "they're playing our tune"
And love is suddenly here to stay.

Plain song, middle years, fighting for careers,
How little time to hear the poems song,
Older, wiser now, listen to the birds,
Their song sweeter than all our words.

Evensong, twilight years,
Moments of quiet joy,
Abide with me, these fondest hours,
No more to prove; just smell the flowers.

Last hymn I shall not hear,
But you'll be there and so will I,
Much nearer than you will know,
Close enough to blow,
A zephyr of a kiss,
To you,
For all our years of bliss.

Whisper on the Village Green

Conceived by love, born without a choice,
Of temperament or disposition,
The outcome of a love affair,
It wasn't your decision.
From a tiny embryo,
Ancestral bloodlines flow,
Your make up, your chemistry,
Genetic strains you'll never know.
Courage bred in the bone,
It's not taught at home.
Introvert or extrovert,
You cannot choose between,
Some find the richest seam in life,
While others only dream.

So carefully weighed when we are born,
No one measures thickness of skin,
Only you will know your heart's on your sleeve,
Or armour-plated within.
Born sensitive, there is no cure,
Build a fence that none shall hurt you,
Then find a love that's pure,
And you'll gain another's virtue.

Sincerity, not learned at school,
Some born to play the fool or act the part,
Behind a shell no one else can tell.

Ambitious, capricious,
It's the rub of the green,
Wise or wild, kind or mean,
There's no choice, it's in the gene.

So life is just a lottery,
You are just what you are,
There was no lucky star,
Don't ask the reason why,
Or how your life is seen.
A hundred years from now,
You'll be a whisper on the village green,
And no one there to know,
Who you were or what you might have been.

Fate

Through all our tender, happy years,
I often ruminate,
How ten thousand miles apart,
The winds of fate,
Blew two seeds to fall
And germinate,
Two young hearts, different as can be,
But there's a chemistry you cannot see
Armed with truth and love alone,
How can I ever repay,
The destiny we found the day,
I walked into the sunny uplands of your smile.